THE CUTE BOOK OF KAWAII COLORING

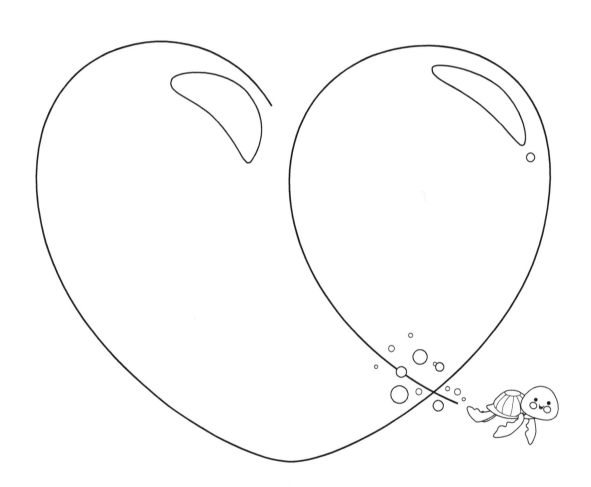

Woo! Jr. Kids Activities Founder: Wendy Piersall

Book Layout by: Michael Koch
Cover Illustration: Michael Koch
Translations: Yoshi Asano

Published by DragonFruit, an imprint of Mango Publishing, a division of Mango Publishing Group, Inc.

For permission requests, please contact the publisher at:

Mango Publishing Group
2850 Douglas Road, 2nd Floor
Coral Gables, FL 33134 USA
info@mango.bz

For special orders, quantity sales, course adoptions and corporate sales, please email the publisher at sales@mango.bz. For trade and wholesale sales, please contact Ingram Publisher Services at customer.service@ingramcontent.com or +1.800.509.4887.

The Cute Book of Kawaii Coloring: Learn Japanese Words by Coloring Cute Things

ISBN: 978-1-64250-703-4

Kawaii is a style of cartoon drawing that originated in Japan. In this book, you'll find lots of fun kawaii-style artwork to color!

 Plus, explore easy-to-learn Japanese words, translations, and special ways to write them!

In each case, there is an English word translated into three types of Japanese writing: Romaji, Hiragana, and Katakana.

The following symbols will represent the English word and each form of Japanese translation:

☆ English
☁ Romaji
□ Hiragana
✧ Katakana

☆	tiger
☁	tora
□	とら
✧	トラ

～ FOR EXAMPLE

Both Hiragana and Katakana characters can usually be created with 3 or 4 strokes. Give it a try!

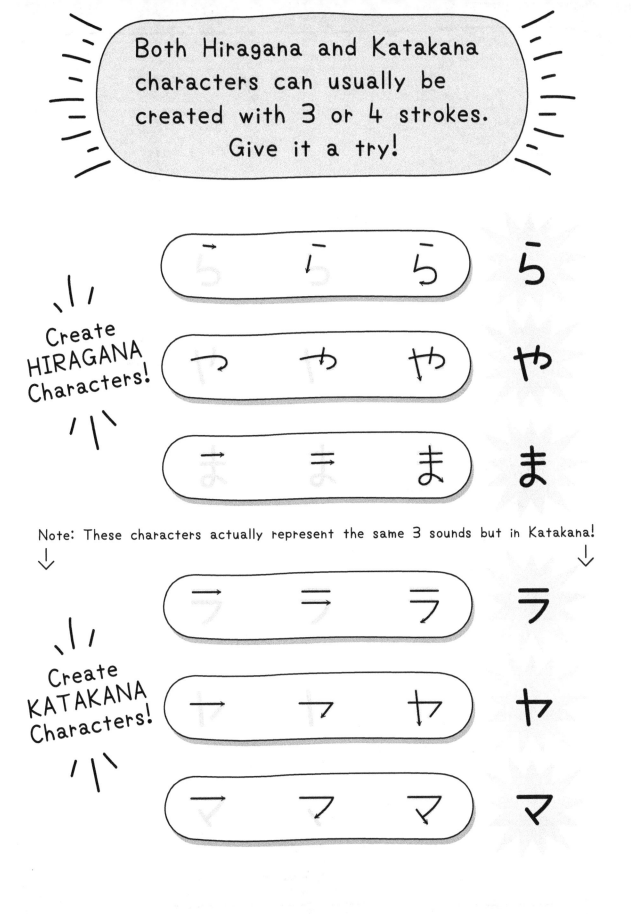

Create HIRAGANA Characters!

ら

や

ま

Note: These characters actually represent the same 3 sounds but in Katakana!

Create KATAKANA Characters!

ラ

ヤ

マ

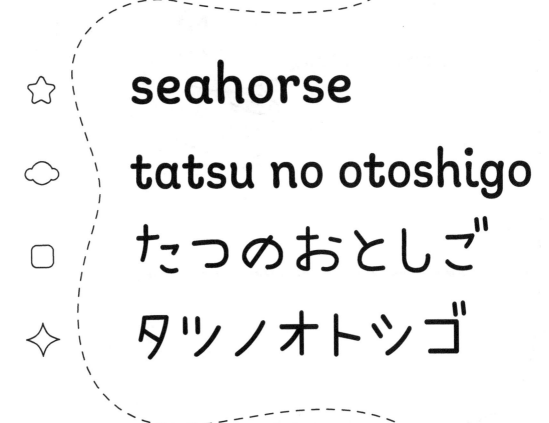

seahorse

tatsu no otoshigo

たつのおとしご

タツノオトシゴ

whale

kujira

くじら

クジラ

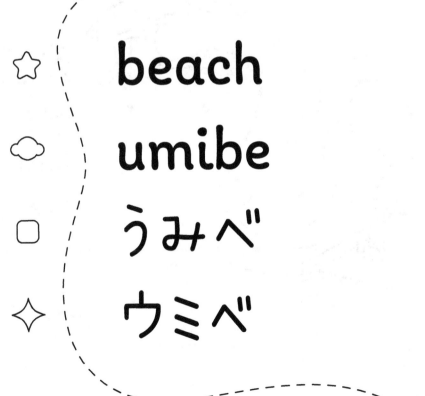

beach

umibe

うみべ

ウミベ

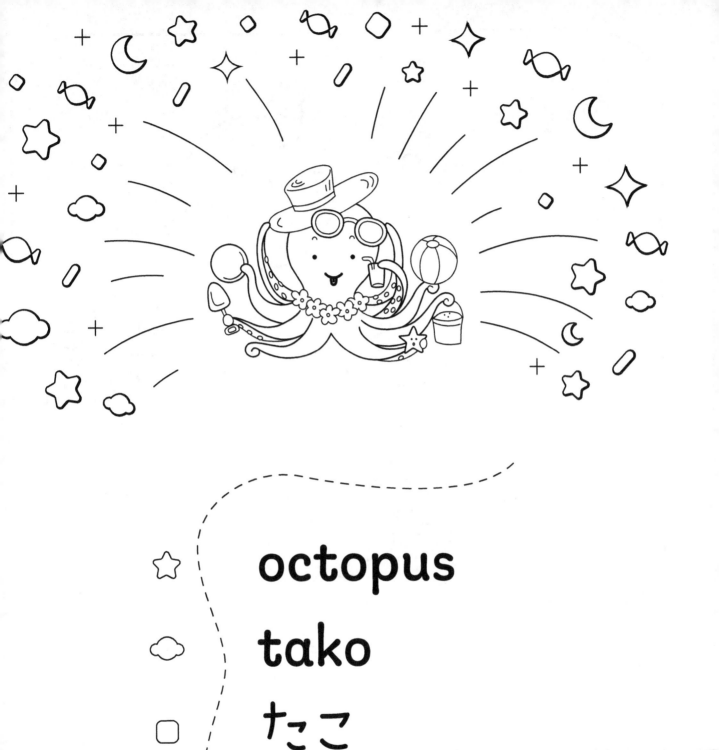

octopus

tako

たこ

タコ

mermaid

ningyo

にんぎょ

ニンギョ

rocket

roketto

ろけっと

ロケット

castle

oshiro

おしろ

オシロ

honeybee

mitsubachi

みつばち

ミツバチ

pirate

kaizoku

かいぞく

カイゾク

sweets

suiitsu

すいーつ

スイーツ

frog

kaeru

かえる

カエル

porcupine

yama arashi

やまあらし

ヤマアラシ

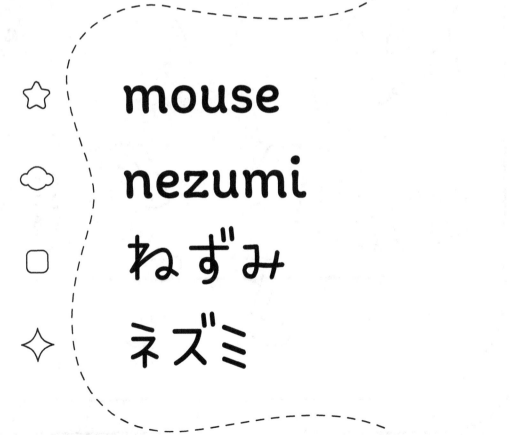

mouse

nezumi

ねずみ

ネズミ

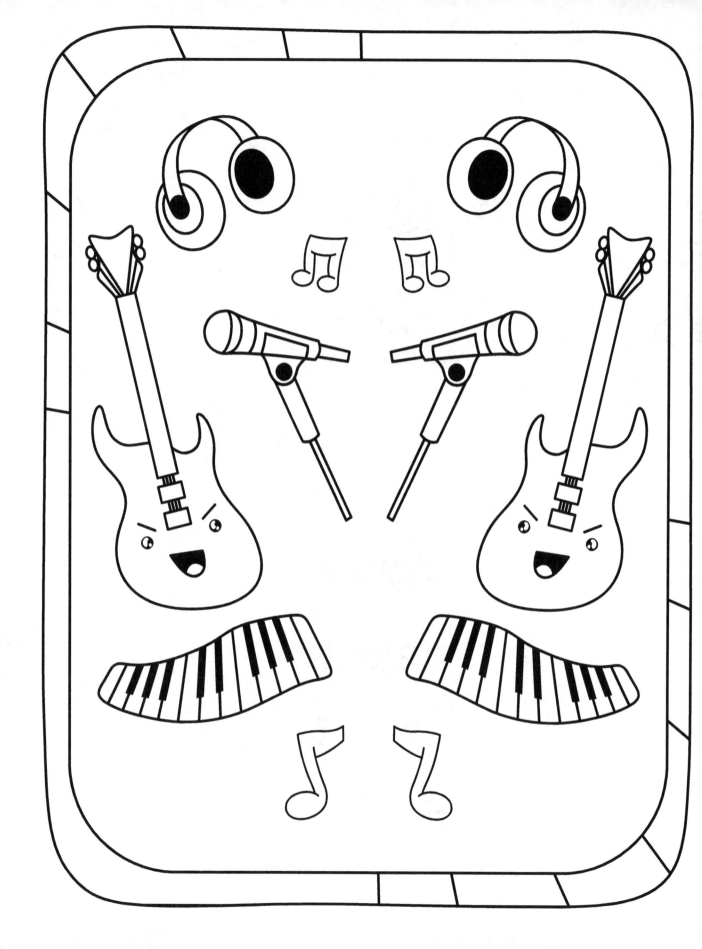

guitar

gitaa

ぎたー

ギター

zebra

shimauma

しまうま

シマウマ

kangaroo

kangaruu

かんがるー

カンガルー

owl

fukuroo

ふくろう

フクロウ

hamburger

hanbaagaa

はんばーがー

ハンバーガー

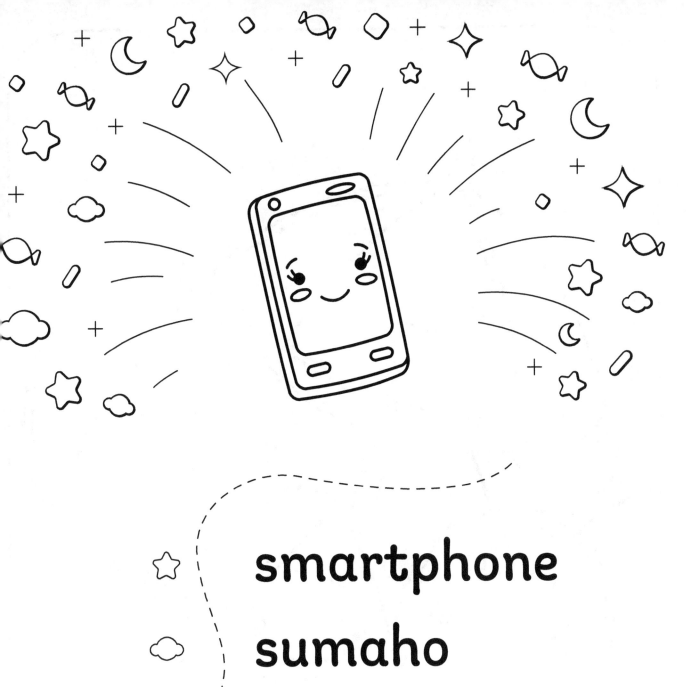

smartphone

sumaho

すまほ

スマホ

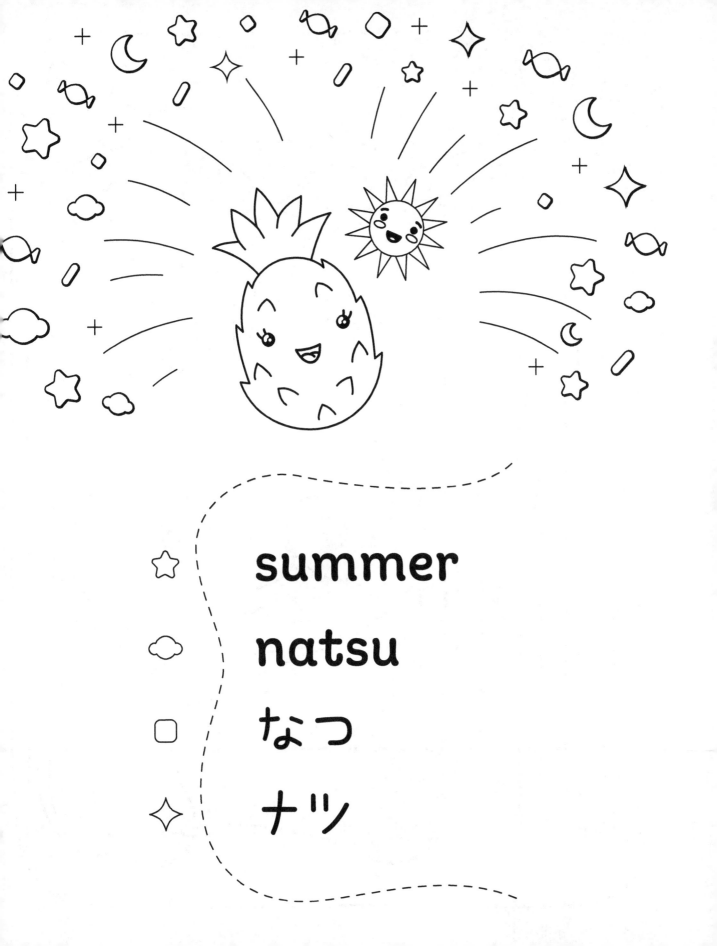

summer

natsu

なつ

ナツ

panda

panda

ぱんだ

パンダ

tiger

tora

とら

トラ

monkey

saru

さる

サル

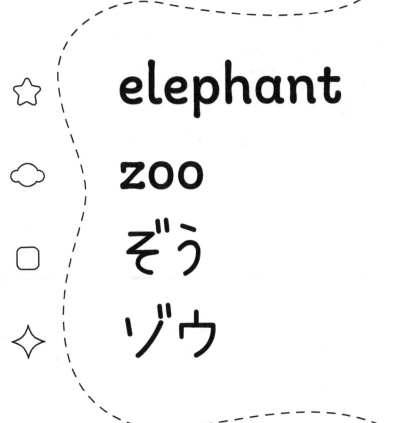

elephant

zoo

ぞう

ゾウ

lizard

tokage

とかげ

トカゲ

girl

onnna no ko

おんなのこ

オンナノコ

butterfly

choocho

ちょうちょ

チョウチョ

dinosaur

kyooryuu

きょうりゅう

キョウリュウ

dragon

ryuu

りゅう

リュウ

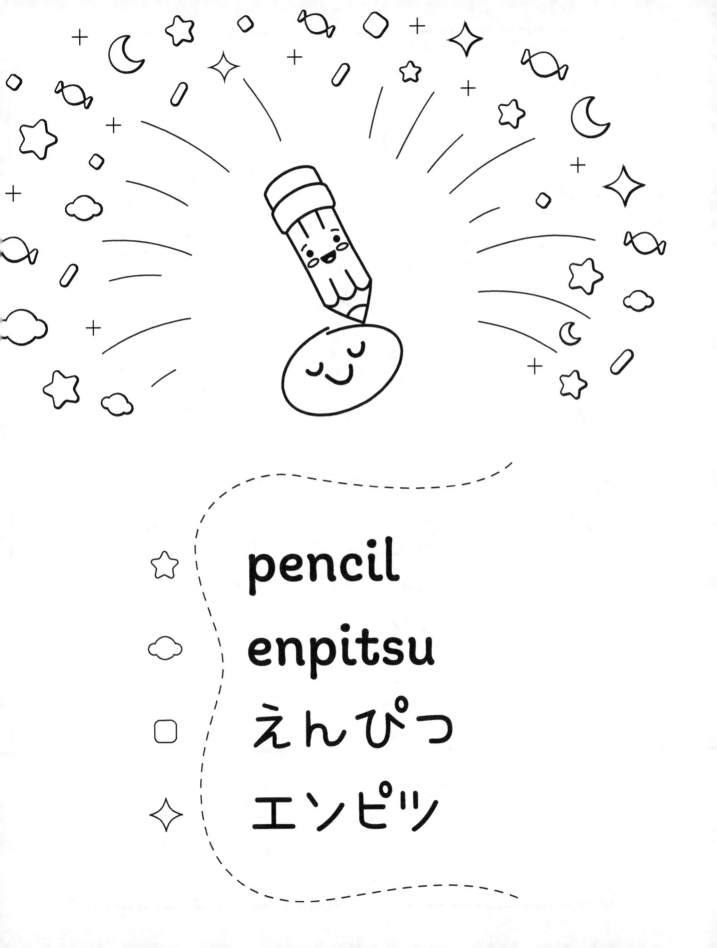

pencil

enpitsu

えんぴつ

エンピツ

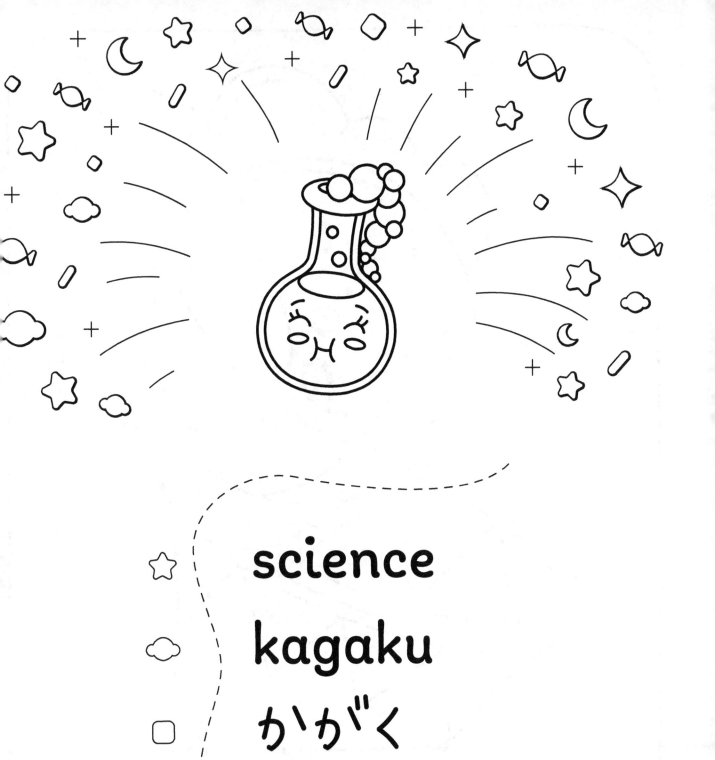

science

kagaku

かがく

カガク

basketball

basukettobooru

ばすけっとぼーる

バスケットボール

football

futtobooru

ふっとぼーる

フットボール

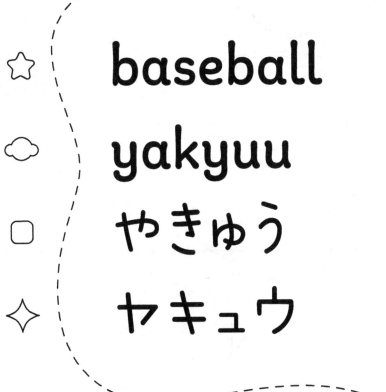

baseball

yakyuu

やきゅう

ヤキュウ

hockey

hokkee

ほっけー

ホッケー

tennis

tenisu

てにす

テニス

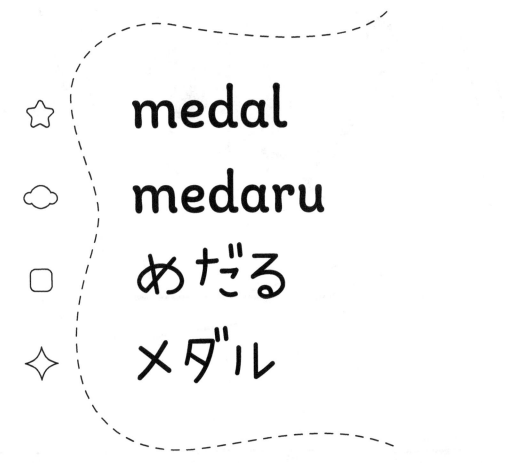

medal

medaru

めだる

メダル

backpack

bakkupakku

ばっくぱっく

バックパック

book

hon

ほん

ホン

drum

taiko

たいこ

タイコ

sea turtle

umigame

うみがめ

ウミガメ

dolphin

iruka

いるか

イルカ

cat

neko

ねこ

ネコ

giraffe

kirin

きりん

キリン

bear

kuma

くま

クマ

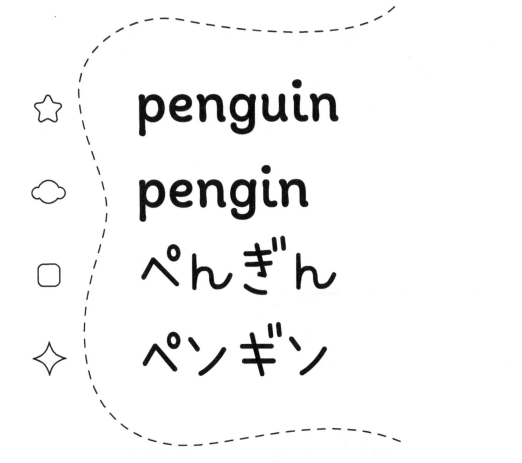

penguin

pengin

ぺんぎん

ペンギン

pig

buta

ぶた

ブタ

robot

robotto

ろぼっと

ロボット

☆ koala

☁ koara

▢ こあら

✦ コアラ

rhinoceros

sai

さい

サイ

worm

kemushi

けむし

ケムシ

chicken

niwatori

にわとり

ニワトリ

wolf

ookami

おおかみ

オオカミ

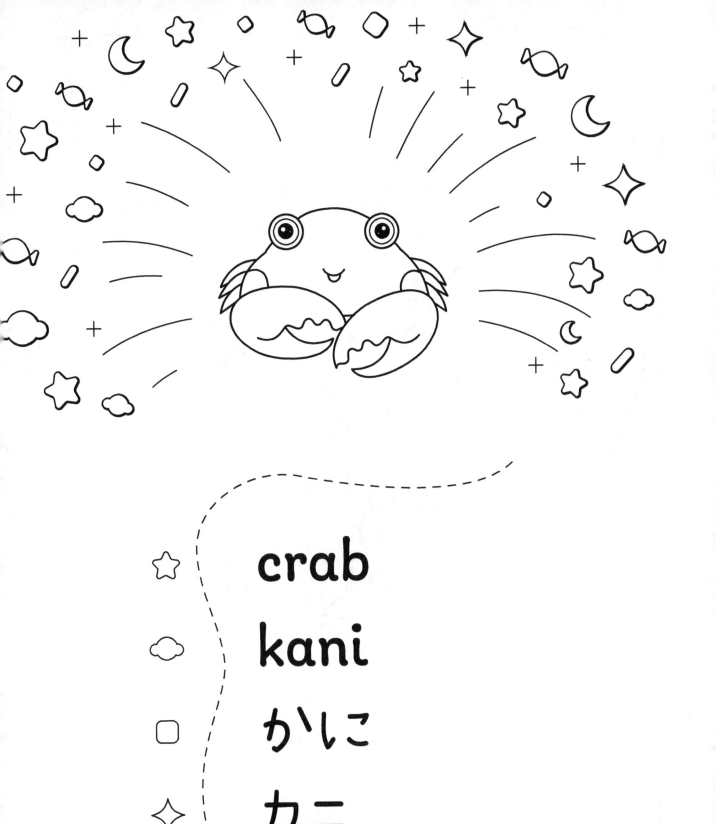

crab

kani

かに

カニ

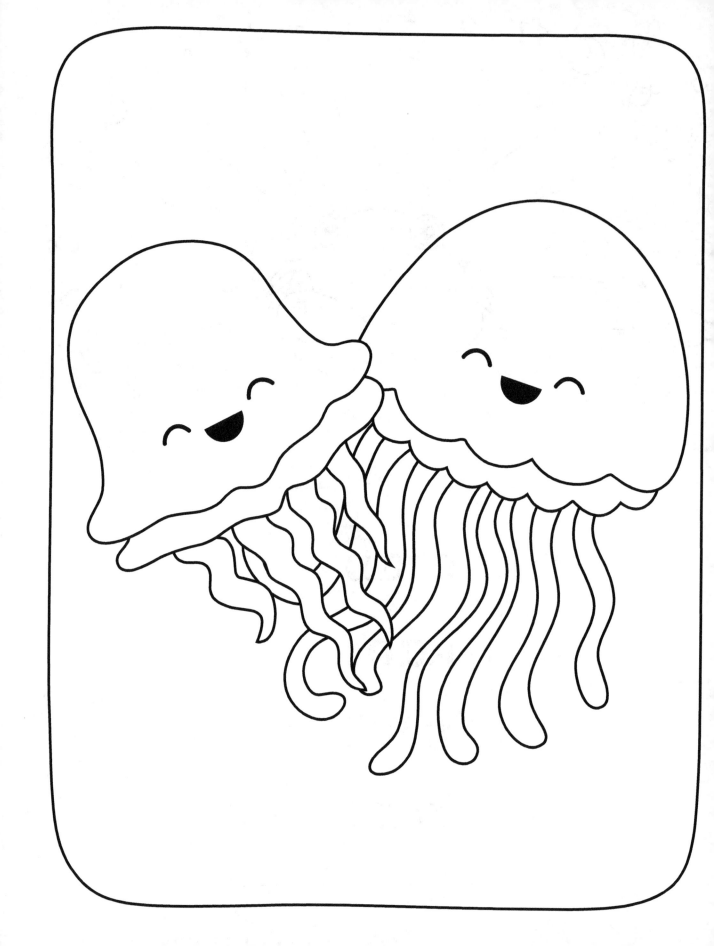

jellyfish

kurage

くらげ

クラゲ

fish

sakana

さかな

サカナ

Woo! Jr. Kids' Activities is passionate about inspiring children to learn through imagination and FUN. That is why we have provided thousands of craft ideas, printables, and teacher resources to over 55 million people since 2008. We are on a mission to produce books that allow kids to build knowledge, express their talent, and grow into creative, compassionate human beings. Elementary education teachers, day care professionals, and parents have come to rely on Woo! Jr. for high-quality, engaging, and innovative content that children LOVE. Our bestselling kids activity books have sold over 375,000 copies worldwide.

Tap into our free kids activity ideas at our website WooJr.com or by following us on social media:

https://www.pinterest.com/woojrkids/
https://www.facebook.com/WooJr/
https://twitter.com/woojrkids
https://www.instagram.com/woojrkids/

DragonFruit, an imprint of Mango Publishing, publishes high-quality children's books to inspire a love of lifelong learning in readers. DragonFruit publishes a variety of titles for kids, including children's picture books, nonfiction series, toddler activity books, pre-K activity books, science and education titles, and ABC books. Beautiful and engaging, our books celebrate diversity, spark curiosity, and capture the imaginations of parents and children alike.

Mango Publishing, established in 2014, publishes an eclectic list of books by diverse authors. We were named the Fastest Growing Independent Publisher by Publishers Weekly in 2019 and 2020. Our success is bolstered by our main goal, which is to publish high-quality books that will make a positive impact in people's lives.

Our readers are our most important resource; we value your input, suggestions, and ideas. We'd love to hear from you—after all, we are publishing books for you!

Please stay in touch with us and follow us at:

Instagram: @dragonfruitkids

Facebook: Mango Publishing

Twitter: @MangoPublishing

LinkedIn: Mango Publishing

Pinterest: Mango Publishing

Sign up for our newsletter at www.mangopublishinggroup.com and receive a free book! Join us on Mango's journey to change publishing, one book at a time.

CPSIA information can be obtained
at www.ICGtesting.com
Printed in the USA
JSHW030532170921
18760JS00009B/11